MY HEART CRIES OUT

LAURA BAILEY-AUBOUG

LAURA BAILEY-AUBOUG

My Heart Cries Out Copyright © January 2019 by Laura Bailey-Auboug. Published in the United States of America by Gospel 4 U Network Publishing department

All rights reserved. No part of this book may be reproduced or transmitted in anyway by means, electronic, mechanical, Photocopy, recording or otherwise, without prior permission of the author except as provided by USA copyright law.

ISBN – 978-0-692-20524-2

Library of Congress Number – 2017904959

Printed in United States of America

January 2019

LAURA BAILEY-AUBOUG

Content

DEDICATION

FOREWORD

ACKNOWLEDGEMENTS

INTRODUCTION

PROLOGUE

The Birth of My Son 21

Kristin's: Diagnosis..................................27

Kristin's Medical Journey............................31

Preschool and Elementary Years.....................51

Middle School and High School Year..................59

Letters Advocating for My Child....................... 65

Poems for Kristin..77

Setbacks... 81

The Family Life and Holidays.......................…84

A Mother's Message................................. 97

Kristin's Gallery

About the Author

Dedication

It is my pleasure to dedicate this book to my wonderful and loving Father, the Almighty God, who gives me the strength and courage to endure this life experience, and for placing the inspiration in me to write and share my testimony.

I also dedicate this book to my first-born son Christopher, who has been with me side by side through all my struggles and depression. To him I say thanks for all his uplifting words of encouragement, bringing me beautiful flowers when I was sad, encouraging me, and keeping me focused while I was going through the storm.

I would also like to dedicate this book to my son Kristin, who has taught me how to be a compassionate, loving, and caring mother.

LAURA BAILEY-AUBOUG

Foreword

My sister's intense, emotional account of her personal struggles raising a special needs child is humbling. My name is Vilma Bailey-Hasan, and I have witnessed the walls she has faced when reaching out for help. For years, I have seen my sister fight for equality in education and services for her disabled son. I have seen her be his biggest advocate in breaking down barriers in order to find the correct educational placement and medical facility—a battle she faced on a daily basis. I have seen her struggle to teach her son to live in a society that has little knowledge about individuals with disabilities, and a society that appears to be so prejudiced towards the disabled that it made me question how that could be possible! But with all of my sister's challenges, I've witnessed the dignity she maintains as she continues to trust in God, knowing He will make a way for her and her child.

Caring for a special needs child is a very difficult journey for my sister. She wants to make a difference in not only her own son's life, but in the lives of other families also facing that wall. Feeling like she was being held back between the public's ignorance on the subject and her own limited medical knowledge, she decided to go back to college and obtained her Master's Degree in Special Education. Now armed with the tools necessary to face her battles, she could actually work in this field and be a true advocate for those who face similar challenges.

My Heart Cries Out is ideal for any parent who has struggled with the inequities and injustices of our current system with trying to find a proper educational program and appropriate healthcare. After reading this book, you will have the courage and knowledge to research and obtain the appropriate services that you would like to have for your special needs child. You will read letters that my sister wrote to numerous schools and facilities advocating for her child to have the education and healthcare that, in her heart, she always knew he should have.

Thank you,

Vilma Bailey-Hasan

Acknowledgement

I would like to acknowledge my husband, François Yves Auboug, who has always been there for me during the preparation of this book, for his companionship and continual support.

I am also thankful for everyone who assisted me and worked diligently in proofreading and helping me put this book together.

Laura Bailey-Auboug

LAURA BAILEY-AUBOUG

Introduction

For years, my son Kristin has struggled with many obstacles and barriers in his life. His struggles began at birth. Kristin was born with a very complex medical disability that includes autism and several other serious medical conditions. Because of his health challenges, he has allergic reactions to several medicines, which make treatment for his many ailments an ongoing struggle. As a special needs infant, raising him was very difficult and took its toll on me, both mentally and physically. As he grew older, caring for him became more and more of a challenge. In addition to struggling with getting adequate healthcare services for Kristin, there was the dilemma of advocating for him to receive the right educational program to attend a specialized private school.

The fact that most hospitals could not care for my son's complex health condition made treatment for him at such institutions very difficult. As the years went by, Kristin's medical problems became more and more complex. He was transferred from one hospital to another, in the hope that the next hospital would be the one that would give him the care he needed.

As a mother, this experience has been a very traumatic one for me. I struggled with coming to terms with my son's medically compromised situation and my inability to get him healed. Throughout this ordeal, one of the scriptures I held on to was, *"...and the peace of God, which surpasses all understanding, will guard your hearts and minds through Christ Jesus."* **(Philippians 4:7)**.

The title of this book, **My Heart Cries Out**, came to me many, many years ago when I was having a very difficult time dealing with my son's numerous medical disabilities. I cried out to God because I had no one else to turn to, and I knew that He alone could heal my broken heart. I cried out to Him every day continuously.

It is my heart's desire that after reading this book, you will be able to inspire a loved one or you will be inspired to seek God while going through the storm, despite any obstacle in your life. I hope that you will have the determination and the inspiration to fight for the rights of your loved ones that cannot defend themselves.

LAURA BAILEY-AUBOUG

Prologue

From the day Kristin was born (well, until today) no one knew the pain that I felt and continue to feel. The thought of writing this book came during one of my many visits to the hospital emergency room. As I sat there waiting for my son to get treated, numerous thoughts flooded my mind. I had so many questions that I needed answers to. There were so many things I wanted to say but didn't know how or when to say them. You see, there is not one day that goes by that I don't think about Kristin. He is so precious to me. He is a very special child and truly a gift from God. His older brother Christopher is also very special to me. However, Kristin's special needs have taken up so much of my time, and I feel guilty that I did not spend enough time with Christopher.

I wanted to share this testimony so that my oldest son could one day read and understand how much I love him and appreciate the incredible amount of support he has given me since he was six years old. I hope he will forgive me for not spending time with him. I want mothers who experience similar situations with special needs children to understand that they are not alone and that, by God's grace, they too can go through the fire and come out victorious. I also want fathers to get a glimpse of the trials mothers endure so that they can step up and play a more pivotal role in the rearing of their children, especially those with special needs.

During my test, I have truly gotten the victory. At one point in this journey, I didn't think that I would have ever stopped crying. Thank God I don't cry as many tears anymore, but my heart still cries out to God. I have grown spiritually, and my relationship with God is so much deeper now. God's grace and mercy comfort me. My heart cries out to God and He hears my daily cries. He continues to deliver me, and He surrounds me with His loving kindness.

My Heart Cries Out

LAURA BAILEY-AUBOUG

~1~

The Birth of My Son

This is a personal story about the birth and life of my second son, Kristin.

At 6:50 a.m. on May 6th, 1990, my son Kristin came into the world. He was born with twelve fingers and twelve toes. I was amazed because that was a bit unusual to me. I had never heard of a child being born with so many fingers and toes. Kristin's aunt was present at the time of his birth, and she was also amazed to see him with twelve fingers and twelve toes. But even with so many fingers and toes, he was precious. To me, he was beautiful, and I saw no fault in him. He was my baby and when he looked at me, his eyes said, "Mommy, I want to live." When I looked at him, I saw a perfect gift from God.

James 1:17 says: "*Every good gift and every perfect gift is from above, and comes down from the Father of lights, with whom there is no variation or shadow of turning.*"

On May 7th, his second day, I realized that something was wrong with him. He was not drinking his milk or opening his mouth. I brought my concerns to the nurses and one of them reassured me that he was fine and that newborn babies normally had problems with their drinking. Shortly after talking to the nurse and getting her reassurance, my deepest fears were realized. The doctor came into my room and informed me that my baby was very ill and had to be transferred to a neonatal unit at a specialized hospital. I was devastated, and I cried and cried. I ran over to his little crib and I held and kissed him. I didn't want to let him go. I cried as I held him, and my tears were running all over his little face. His bright eyes kept staring at me as though he wanted me to know that everything would be alright. My heart was broken as the doctor took him away. I began to cry louder and louder. As I stood there helplessly watching my baby being taken away, I felt that my insides were being ripped out from within me. My broken heart cried out. With every teardrop that fell, every ounce of my energy and strength seemed to drain out of me. My soul seemed weak. I was in pain and I certainly was in distress. And then, I began to pray, "Lord, help my baby."

Immediately, I asked my doctor to discharge me from the hospital so that I could be with my baby. My doctor was very hesitant to discharge me at first, fearing that after just hearing the news about my son, I was not in a logical state of mind. I began to plead with her, telling her that I could not stay in this hospital while my baby was in another hospital. She finally agreed, and I was discharged.

Within an hour of my discharge, I went straight to the neonatal unit and asked the nurse in charge to see my child. To my dismay, the nurse informed me that my baby was not there. I tried explaining to the nurses that my baby was transferred to this hospital, but they insisted that he was not there. Then it was confirmed by the doctor that my son had indeed been transferred to the neonatal unit.

When I finally saw Kristin, it was a terrible sight to behold. He was placed in an incubator and there were needles all over his tiny body. His eyes were banded to protect him from the light and he seemed so helpless. I asked the nurse if I could hold him and she said that I could for only five minutes. As I held him I began to cry, and my heart cried out to God. The nurse then informed me that he must be placed back into the incubator. The five minutes went by so quickly that it felt like five seconds.

I had to wait one week before my son could be seen by a neurologist and other specialists. During the following three weeks at that hospital, Kristin had seen several doctors and specialists. After meeting with the entire team of specialists, they all had discouraging words to say about my son's condition. The worst news came from his brain specialist, who informed me that, because of the complexity of my son's condition, he may not live past four weeks. Again, I cried. I cried every day and every night. I sat and wondered day after day what would happen to Kristin. My heart cried out to God but, while I respected the doctors' knowledge and relied on them to help my baby get well, I refused to believe their bad news. I knew that only God had the last say in everything. As the days went on, my faith in God grew stronger and I prayed for a miracle.

God's Word says, *"The eyes of the Lord are upon the righteous, and his ears are open unto their cry."* **(Psalm 34:15)**

I visited my son at the hospital every day. Many days I would arrive at 7:00 a.m. and leave the hospital at around 11:30 p.m. Every time I saw him, he seemed to be so helpless. The nurse had to put a tube through his tiny nostril to feed him. I hated feeding time because the tube looked so painful. On occasions when he was fed, I would ask the nurse over and over if the feeding tube was painful and she would reply that babies do not feel the pain. But as a mother, watching my newborn being fed with a tube through his nostril, I felt the pain for him and for me. I'd leave the room often during feeding time because I would cry relentlessly.

As the weeks went by and the fourth week was approaching, I asked God to please not let Kristin die. God had a perfect plan for my son. Kristin was discharged within one month. As I walked into the hospital to receive him, my heart was beating faster and faster. I kept hoping that he would be coming home in good health. The thought of what the neurologist and other specialists had said to me about children that were born with his condition not living past four weeks kept coming back to my memory over and over. I was so afraid; tears were running down my face. I had reached the neonatal unit and, as I got closer to his incubator, I could not believe my eyes! I saw the nurse feeding him with a bottle! The nurse then brought him to me and my heart cried out! I squeezed him and kissed him about a million times.

I never cried so much in my life before Kristin's birth. When I learned about Kristin's condition, I knew the journey would be long and painful. However, nowhere in my thoughts, conscious or otherwise, did I anticipate that the journey would be this painful. There were countless times when I cried out all my tears. I was crying but there were no more tears to fall. I remember enduring moments of pain, weakness, and sadness only God could understand. My heart cried out! But I remembered that God's Word says, *"My grace is sufficient for you, for my strength is made perfect in weakness."* **(2 Corinthians 12:6)**

LAURA BAILEY-AUBOUG

~2~
Kristin's Diagnosis

My son Kristin was born May 6th, 1990, in Philadelphia, PA, with autism and a very complex disability known as the 22q11.2 deletion syndrome. This diagnosis includes the following disorders:

- Pervasive developmental disorders-active
- Chronic ITP-Evans syndrome
- Pulmonary valve disorder
- Bicuspid aortic valve; first degree heart block
- First degree heart block
- Varicella uncomplicated
- Di-George's syndrome
- Clinical Alert-needs repeat CBC prior to suture removal
- Headache

☐ CHR SEROUS OM SIMP/NOS

According to The Children's Hospital of Philadelphia (CHOP), the 22q11.2 deletion syndrome has only recently gained attention. Although the Di-George and Velocardiofacial syndromes are not newly recognized, it is only during the past decade that the two have been identified as one and the same, originating from a unique deletion on chromosome 22q. Through the advent of Florescent in Situ Hybridization (FISH) analysis, diagnosis of these syndromes has become widely available.

The 22q11.2 deletion is a chromosomal difference, which is the result of a small piece of chromosome 22 not being present. There are approximately 27 genes in the region which are missing. Research has identified which genes are missing but it has not yet discovered what role the genes play in the development and which genes play the most important roles. Most children with the 22q11.2 deletion have the same piece of DNA missing despite the wide spectrum of presentation in the children. The 22q11.2 deletion can result in a variety of problems, including but not limited to heart defects, immune system dysfunction, hypocalcemia, palate problems, feeding difficulties, kidney differences, difficulties in school, and learning disabilities. The 22q11.2 deletion has a region of the genome which is structurally less stable, and thus the piece of chromosome 22 simply falls out. The 22q11.2 deletion is thought to occur in approximately 1 in 4,000 live births. For individuals with the 22q11.2 deletion, the recurrence risk is 50%.

Further research led by CHOP shows that nearly every system of the body is at risk for abnormalities with this diagnosis. Patients receiving care at facilities not familiar with the syndrome are not likely to receive optimal treatment. We now recognize that reactions to medications are not typical and that learning and behavioral patterns are unique. Problems are likely to be missed and then mistreated if not identified by experienced specialists. Source: The Children's Hospital of Philadelphia.

LAURA BAILEY-AUBOUG

~3~

Kristin's Medical Journey

The day had finally come; my baby was home and all I had to do was take care of God's precious gift. My entire family came over to see him that day. He was so beautiful and precious; a mother's dream. At six weeks old, my maternity leave was up, and I had to go back to work. Kristin's aunt willingly and lovingly cared for him while I was at work. Even though I had to wrench myself away from him each workday, I knew he was in good hands. Kristin's complex condition has scared me many times. Bringing him home was the beginning of many hospitalizations, many near misses and many, many bouts of bad news. As the days, weeks, and months went by, he developed more medical problems. For the next eleven months of his tender life, we journeyed to and from the doctors' offices and hospitals for his treatment and for their observation of his progress. It seemed that my son was poked and prodded at least twice a month. Then Kristin had his first major surgery at the tender age of one year old and he was placed under general anesthesia.

At eighteen months he had developed bruising under his skin. I was so afraid to take him to the hospital, fearing that the doctors might accuse me of child abuse. Nevertheless, I put my fears aside and trusted God. So, with the Word of God planted deep within my soul, I took him to the hospital. When I arrived at the emergency room and explained to the doctors that Kristin had developed bruising under his skin even though he did not fall or injure himself, the doctors gave me a very suspicious look and started speaking to each other. I further explained to them that my son was born very ill with many major complications and had been hospitalized several times since birth. One of the doctors drew his blood for analysis.

Kristin's older brother accompanied me to the hospital that time. As we sat there together, the wait seemed to go on forever. So many thoughts and memories invaded my mind: Kristin's birth, finding out how sick he truly was, the doctors' prognosis that he may not live past four weeks, his surgery six months before, our many visits to the hospital, this unexplained bruising of his skin, and now, the impending results of his blood test. My head was spinning with those thoughts. None seemed positive or better than the other. I felt like I was losing my mind. I was in distress. I held both of my sons in my arms and then I talked to God. I begged Him to let everything be okay.

When the wait was finally over, and the results came back, it was not the news that I had hoped for. The doctor took me to a private room and told me that Kristin had developed Thrombocytopenia. I did not know what that word meant, but my gut told me that, whatever it meant, it was not good news. I began to cry. I looked down at Christopher's face; he was also aware that his baby brother was sick, and he was crying too. Kristin was admitted into the hospital that very same day. Kristin's brother and I both stayed in the hospital with him. We both would not leave him because we loved him very much. We stayed in the hospital for a week and when he was discharged, we were all happy again. It struck me then that this was not only Kristin's and my problem, but Kristin's brother was also affected by this. My heart cried out to God, and then I began to pray to God to help Kristin.

Two years later, Kristin had another emergency room visit because he was bruising again and having problems breathing. The doctor took an X-ray of his lungs and ran some bloodwork. After about five hours in the emergency room, the head doctor came to me and said that he discovered that Kristin had abnormal platelet counts and they immediately admitted him in the hospital. The following day, his grandmother and aunt came to visit him. This gave me a chance to go home, get some rest, and return to spend the night with him. That night was full of pain and tears for both Kristin and me. At 9:00 p.m., the nurse came in to take blood from him, but she had trouble getting his blood from his vein and had to stick him five times. He was screaming and writhing in pain. At 1:00 a.m., the nurse put an IV into his hands and connected him to the monitor. Then around 3:00 a.m. that same morning, as the nurse came to check on his heart rate, he woke up and began to cry. I sat there with him and consoled him until he fell back to sleep at around 4:45 a.m. It was at that moment that I thought about writing about Kristin's journey. Kristin spent eight days in the hospital this time, and when it was time for him to be discharged, I was filled with nothing but joy. Nevertheless, he had several doctor and specialist visits throughout that year.

That same year, Kristin had his blood drawn by his doctor for testing. The next day, I received a call from his doctor informing me that the results from Kristin's test showed that his blood count was very low, and he needed to be immediately admitted to the hospital for a blood transfusion. As soon as I arrived at the hospital with Kristin, he was immediately transfused. But after that transfusion, his blood count went down further. Even after receiving a second transfusion, his blood count remained at the same level. The doctors were worried because his blood level would not go up. One of the head doctors decided to give him steroids but, to the doctor's surprise and my dismay, his blood count went down even more. While sitting in the room with Kristin, his hematologist came to talk to me with tears in her eyes. She advised me that she and the team had tried everything to increase his blood count, but to no avail. Not knowing what else to do, she then apologized to me for not being able to help him. Right then I knew that I could not cry tears, but my heart cried out. I asked God to save my child because I knew when the doctors could not do anymore for my son that it was God's turn to take over. The Bible says that *"God is our refuge and strength, an ever-present help in trouble."* **(Psalm 46:1).**

After praying and crying out to God, my faith became stronger. I had to believe that God was going to increase his blood count. I prayed for a miraculous healing. The following morning, he had his blood count check. As the technician took his blood, I was praying silently. God heard my prayer and He answered me. When the results came back, Kristin's blood count had miraculously risen high enough for him to be discharged. I praised God all the way home and continued my praises for the rest of the day.

Six months after being released, Kristin was back into the hospital for a low blood count. For that entire day and night, I was restless. Over and over, I sat down then walked about and I wondered and hoped for a miracle. I even prayed for what he was going through to be only a long dream, a dream that would soon come to an end. Unfortunately for Kristin and me, that dream was our reality. I realized that rather than wish it away, I had to face the harsh truth that my son was very ill and needed healing. Despite all the bad reports, I still put my trust in God. I cried to God silently and I know that God heard my cries. When he was discharged from the hospital that time, I was happy again. That day was a very joyful moment for both him and his brother. As he began to grow, more challenging medical problems would arise.

At the age of three, Kristin was in the care of his aunt, whom he loved dearly. She realized that his heart was beating fast. She brought it to my attention and advised me to take him to the emergency room. I thought that she was overreacting and didn't think much of it. Nevertheless, since she had been so close to him and had knowledge of his medical condition, I decided to take him to the emergency room just to please her. When I arrived at the hospital, to my surprise, he was taken immediately to be checked by the nurse. Suddenly, a doctor came to me and informed me that he needed to have another blood transfusion immediately. I was in shock when the doctor further stated that if he hadn't come into the hospital he would not have survived the following day. I cried and cried because I didn't want him to have another blood transfusion. My heart cried out to God and I knew he heard me.

God's Word says, *"Oh, taste and see that the Lord is good; Blessed is the man who trusts in Him!"* **(Psalm 34:8)**

This time, he stayed in the hospital for five days and all I could do was cry. I believe that I grew closer to God during that time because there was no one to talk to but God, and I know that God alone hears my cries. When he was discharged, I held him in my arms. I wanted to cry but the tears could not come, and I knew that my heart was crying. When I took him home, I monitored him closely. Every time he would visit the doctor I became afraid, not knowing what would happen or what to expect next with his health. My child's life was like a rollercoaster. One day he was fine, and the next day he was at the doctor. That year I took a leave of absence from my job to take better care of him. I stayed home for about six weeks with him and when it was time for me to return to work, I became very saddened. His aunt, who lived with us, took care of him again. I trusted her because she was so good with him. As a matter of fact, she would know when he was about to get sick before I did.

When Kristin was four, I began working the night shift so that I could spend time with Kristin during the day. While at work around 4:00 a.m., I received a frantic and nervous call from Kristin's caregiver, his grandmother. She said to me, "You have to come home right now. I called the ambulance for Kristin because he is having problems breathing; they are working on him now in the ambulance."

Without a thought, I jumped into my car and headed to the hospital. To this day, I have no recollection of leaving work or arriving at the hospital. What I do remember is being next to him in the emergency room, where the doctors were giving him oxygen. His face and eyes were full of tears. He kept staring at me as though he was trying to tell me something. I felt helpless, guilty, and angry. If only I was at home with him, this would have never occurred. If only I had quit this stupid job and given him all my attention. As all these thoughts ran through my mind, I asked God, "Why, Lord?"

Six months after being discharged, I took Kristin for a pre-operation appointment. During our consultation, he began to have a seizure. All I saw was his eyes rolling back in their sockets and I thought that this time for certain, he was going to die. I was so helpless and grew scared as the seizure worsened. I began to cry and pray for God to save my child. In what seemed like a split second, he was rushed down to the emergency room and a team of doctors attended to him. They admitted him, and again he spent a couple of days in the hospital. When they discharged him, my fears turned to joy once again, and I gave God the praise. **Psalm 145:2** tells us: *"While I live I will praise the Lord; I will sing praises to my God while I have my being."*

At the age of nine, Kristin had a dentist appointment. The dentist forgot to check his blood prior to cleaning his teeth. As the dentist began the procedure on Kristin's tooth, Kristin began to bleed. The dentist got scared because he could not stop the blood from flowing. The dentist then called in the chief dentist, who also could not contain the bleeding. As Kristin lay on the chair, he began to get weaker and weaker. The dentist called in Kristin's hematologist, who immediately began to give him a blood transfusion; Kristin spent about five days at the hospital and was discharged when his blood count went up. To God be the glory.

Throughout this experience, my emotions seemed to be a never-ending rollercoaster. On the days that Kristin thrived, I was thankful, happy, and filled with joy and peace within my heart. I had every reason to give God all the praise He so rightly deserves. Then there were days when my son fell ill, and I found no strength or courage to deal with the challenges of his illnesses. I knew my faith in God would see me through, and it did. Unfortunately, my emotions were not always positive. There were days when I felt angry, bitter, frustrated, confused, lonely, helpless, and downright hopeless. One year when Kristin had multiple hospitalizations, I was overwhelmed with the amount of suffering that Kristin had endured and became very stressed out and depressed. I felt that I had failed him as a mother. Instead of bringing into the world a healthy and happy-go-lucky, normal baby, I had betrayed him. I brought him into this world to suffer through multiple illnesses, countless hospitalizations, and surgeries with no relief in sight, and there was nothing I could do to make him better. What was even more debilitating was that I felt very guilty for neglecting his brother. Caring for Kristin took so much of my time and energy that I had very little of me left for Christopher. I was failing him too. There is no worse feeling than to feel that you have failed your children. I cried and cried again, feeling weak and crying hopelessly on my bed, and a voice said to me, "Why don't you end your life?" I knew that it was the devil, but I had no strength to resist him. I got up from my bed as if in a trance and walked to my dresser, where my allergy medications were. I emptied the bottle of pills in my hand and was about to swallow every one of them. Just at that moment, I heard a tiny knock on my door and a voice saying, "Mom, it's me, open, I have something for you!" With trembling hands, I put the pills back in the bottle and opened the door. There was my first-born, Christopher, with a handful of beautiful flowers for me. After that close encounter with death, I learnt that I must guard my heart always, keep it pure, and never let the devil plant any negative seeds in my mind. I fell to my knees in repentance. I began to pray and thank God for my life.

I believe that God used Kristin's brother to interrupt what the devil had planned for me that day. Since that moment, I have never, ever had a thought like that again and I became closer to God. I still have daily challenges with Kristin's condition, but my hopelessness has been replaced with strength, faith, and the firm belief that God has me, and my family, covered with His blood. No matter what comes my way, I am at peace in my Savior's arms and my heart is filled with faith and promise. He continues to guide me, and an unspeakable joy abounds around me now.

God's Word says, *"For this is God Our God forever and ever; He will be our guide Even to death."* (**Psalm 47: 14**)

You may have heard this saying a thousand times, but I will say it again because it is very true. The devil's assignment on this earth is to steal, kill, and destroy, but he is a liar! God in His infinite mercy had a perfect plan for my life. I know now that God put me through these tests so that I can share my testimony with others who feel alone and hopeless as I once did. God has a perfect plan for your life too. Get to know Him. Trust and believe in Him and His Word. I promise that He will direct your path to victory. We may still go through pain and suffering, but God will see us through.

Prior to Kristin's 15th birthday, Kristin was hospitalized approximately over 24 times and it just got worse for Kristin. He began to develop allergic reactions to a lot of the medicine that was prescribed and started hallucinating. He was admitted to the hospital and placed on high restriction. It was extremely hard for him, and he was very scared. There were various incidents which I considered abuse. On one occasion, I came to visit Kristin and he was sound asleep and was put into a 4-point restraint and tied to the bed. I stayed in the room for about a half hour and no one came to check on him. I then informed the head nurse that he was asleep and still tied to the bed, since the rules are, if the child falls asleep the restraints must be off, but that never occurred with my child. On another occasion he accidentally had spilled his food and the aide who was there to monitor him got angry and threw his food away. These are just a few incidents, but Kristin had many other horrible, painful hospital experiences, many of which I have blocked out because they were too painful. Despite what I was going through with my son, I knew that God would not give me more than I could handle.

Kristin spent his 15th birthday at the hospital. I brought him a cake and celebrated his birthday with family members. His aunt and cousins came and visited him every day. As the holidays approached, I would often wonder if he would be coming home. Not only did Kristin have support from his family, but our pastor and members at our church visited him. They would come, sit, and pray with him. During one of his three-month stays at a mental institution, Kristin began to have seizures. So, he was transferred to a medical hospital for children and stayed for one week. Then he had to be transferred to a specialized hospital in Virginia.

Prior to transferring Kristin to the hospital in Virginia, it was a battle fighting with the insurance company to have him transferred out of state. They wanted him to be placed in a hospital in Pennsylvania, but there were no hospitals in Pennsylvania that could treat his complex medical problems. In addition to Kristin's numerous medical problems, he also had developed physiological, behavioral, and emotional problems. This made his treatment very complex. When one hospital treated his medical problem, unfortunately, they were unable to treat his psychological, emotional, and behavioral problems. This hospital in

Virginia was highly recommended as the best that could treat his condition. Again, I had to submit letters to various agencies informing them that it was medically necessary for my son to be transferred to that specialized hospital in Virginia. Eventually, they honored my request and approved his referral to be admitted at that specialized hospital in Virginia.

The following day we had to get him ready for the five-hour ride in the ambulance, from one hospital to another. When I walked into his hospital room, while he awaited transfer to the specialized hospital in Virginia, he asked me if he was going home. I didn't want to have to tell him that he was not on his way home but to yet another hospital. When I eventually told him, his eyes filled with tears and we both began to cry. The thought of my baby going all the way to Virginia, where I wouldn't be able to see him every day, made me sad.

God's Word says:

"Cast all your anxiety on Him, because He cares for you." **(1Peter 5:7)**

Upon our arrival at the Virginia hospital, I noticed the hospital environment looked like a resort. There were big trees, beautiful rocks in front of the building, and a beautiful garden with flowers growing. The nurses and doctors were wonderful. They were kind and caring. They truly showed love to both Kristin and to me. The doctors tried several medicines with Kristin, but he continued to have various allergic reactions. I would call and talk to the nurses almost every day to get updated information about him. Every weekend Kristin's stepdad and I would take the long journey to Virginia to visit him. When the time had come for Kristin to be discharged from the hospital, I was so happy. I cried tears of joy, but the joy turned into sadness when I thought of him coming back to Philadelphia to receive the less than mediocre services he had before.

To my surprise, when he returned to Philadelphia, all his services were discontinued. He could not see his doctors for meds and he had no therapeutic support staff (TSS). He had absolutely nothing. He began to regress. I could not sleep because he would be up at night. He would not eat or drink anything. I called his insurance company, his doctors, and social workers, but no one helped because he had no insurance. He then began to have seizures and ended up back in the Children's Hospital. The emotional pain I felt for him was devastating. Not only was it emotional pain, but I also began to feel his pain physically.

The Children's Hospital doctors still could not treat his complex medical problems. Then with the help of the wonderful doctors and social workers at the hospital, he was again transferred back to the hospital in Virginia. Now the month of November was approaching, and I was concerned about him not spending Thanksgiving with his family. So, his stepdad and I decided to drive to Virginia to spend the holiday with him.

Once we got to Virginia, the hospital put us up to stay at a nice house for the families of the patients that came from out of state. We stayed for a couple of days with Kristin. We took him out and just enjoyed every moment with him.

Prior to our Thanksgiving visit, his brothers, his aunt, and his little cousin also visited him in Virginia. We took him to Virginia Beach and enjoyed our time with him lying on the beach and enjoying the sun and water. Kristin had a lot of fun and so did we.

When the Thanksgiving holiday visit was over and I had to leave him in Virginia, it was very difficult for me to come back to Philadelphia. It was especially hard because I knew that Christmas was approaching, and Kristin loves Christmas and being around his family. But by the grace of God, I was able to let go of all the sadness that was taking control over me. I know that God is good, and He would never give up on Kristin. I have learned to trust God, even when I am at my weakest point.

God's Word says, *"It is better to trust in the Lord than to put confidence in man, it is better to trust in the Lord than to put confidence in princes."* (**Psalm 118:8-9**)

At the age of twenty-three, Kristin had to be seen by seven different specialists. In December of 2013, he saw an orthopedic doctor, who after examining Kristin had some very disturbing news concerning his health. I was informed by his orthopedic doctor that Kristin has sclerosis and must have surgery. I was also told that his spine was growing into his lungs and it would eventually cause him to stop breathing. I was devastated with that disturbing news about his spine. I cried out to God all over again, and I know that God heard my cry. Kristin's surgery was scheduled for December 27, 2013. The orthopedic doctor explained to me the details of the ten-hour spinal surgery that he was going to perform on Kristin's spine. He would cut from the back of his neck to his tailbone, with eighteen pins inserted into his spine. Prior to his surgery, Kristin's cousin and aunt and other family members donated blood for him, because I didn't want to use the blood from the blood bank at the hospital. After talking to God about his ten-hour surgery and praying with a prayer warrior for God to heal his spine, I decided to cancel his scheduled surgery date. On the morning of December 31st at 7:38 a.m., while Kristin was taking a shower, God performed a miraculous miracle on Kristin's spine. God straightened Kristin's "C" curve spine. Kristin is living proof of God's miraculous healing and miracle. I thank God for the mustard seed faith. I knew for sure that my God is a healer, a deliverer, and God is a mighty God. To God be the glory.

James 5:14-15, tells us: *"Is any sick among you? Let him call for the elders of the church; and let them pray over him, anointing him with oil in the name of the Lord: And the prayer of faith shall save the sick, and the Lord shall raise him up; and if he has committed sins, they shall be forgiven him."*

Recently, at the age of twenty-six, Kristin had to be hospitalized for seven days due to his low blood count and he had three blood transfusions. Despite his seven days in the hospital, he was in a good mood and in good spirits.

Kristin's medical battle continues to consist of regular hospital visits, surgeries, and blood transfusions in the hope to stabilize his complex medical problem.

Ephesians 6:16 tells us: *"Above all, taking the shield of faith, wherewith ye shall be able to quench all the fiery darts of the wicked."*

Prior to publishing this book, I experienced an agonizing, distressing, heart-wrenching, and devastating experience with a doctor that was treating Kristin and a social worker that was working with him at the hospital. I had to incorporate this devastating experience into this book. Although I tried to erase this agonizing experience, my conscience would not allow me to do so, because I know that there are parents that have gone through similar situations with their adult children like I have.

On March 7, 2017, I took Kristin to the emergency room because he was not eating or drinking. Kristin had been on steroids for about four and a half months. He had been experiencing some negative side effects from being off his steroids for two weeks. From the emergency room he was sent to the observation unit. After being in the observation unit for four days, one of the doctors and the social worker decided to discharge him, on March 10, 2017, prior to informing me that Kristin had phenomena and a collapsed lung. I informed both the doctor and the social worker that he was not stable, and I would rather have him stabilized before he was discharged. That Friday night when I left the observation unit after visiting Kristin, I got a call from Kristin's support coordinator. She informed me that the social worker in the observation unit told her that Kristin had been abandoned at the hospital and the social worker decided to send Kristin to a group home the following morning.

My heart felt that it was going to burst. It felt like it was being ripped up into ten thousand pieces. I felt crushed, hurt, and angry. I felt hopeless and helpless. I have cared for him for 26 years, and I would never abandon him. The word abandoned is a very strong word. I called Kristin's aunt at once. She made several calls to everyone that could give me some advice on how to stop the transitioning of Kristin to a group home. Kristin's stepdad and I immediately went back to the hospital to find out what was going on. I asked to speak to the doctor in charge. The doctor in charge informed me that the social worker planned to take Kristin at 10 a.m. on Saturday to a group home. I explained to the doctor that I just found out that very same day that they had made plans to transfer my son to a group home, and that was not the right facility for Kristin, since a group home environment couldn't meet his complex medical needs. I further stated that Kristin's doctor recommended an Intermediate Care Facility for Kristin and not a group home. After pleading to the doctor in charge, she agreed with me that a group home was not the facility for Kristin. She further stated that she would discuss Kristin's case with a team of doctors the following morning.

On Saturday, March 10, 2017, I got to the hospital at 7:15 a.m., feeling helpless and hopeless. I asked to speak to the team doctors. Kristin's aunt, who has always been there for him, showed up shortly after. His aunt informed the attending doctor about Kristin's situation and the plans that the social worker had made to transfer him to a group home. The attending doctor informed his aunt that he canceled the transfer to the group home and that Kristin would not be going. When his aunt informed me of what the doctor had said, I began to cry. I felt a relief, a weight off my shoulders, and I began to breathe normally. As the tears began to fall, this is one time that I felt that I could not stop crying. I began to thank God for all that He has done for me and my son. I also thanked God for his aunt, who was there to hold me and console me, and let me know that I must continue to put my trust in God. His aunt also reassured me that God is in control and everything would be alright. The attending doctor also informed me that he would discuss Kristin's case with the specialists. At around 10 a.m., we met with the psychologist, who also informed us that Kristin would not be going to a group home. Instead, he would be admitted on the meds floor until an Intermediate Care Facility was available to him. **Psalm 34:7-8** tells us: *"The angel of the Lord emcampeth round about them that fear Him, and delivereth them. O taste and see that the Lord is good: blessed is the man that trusteth in him."*

I visited Kristin every day that he was in the hospital. On March 13, 2017, I got a call from Kristin's support coordinator informing me that Kristin was being discharged that very same day, and he would be sent to the same group home which they had planned on sending him previously. I was very devastated and furious. I thought to myself, How can they discharge my son and again make arrangements for him to go to a group home without notifying me? I realized that there must be a breakdown in the system and a major communication problem with the doctors and social worker. I was so upset I began to cry again. I got to the hospital at once to discuss his case with the doctor in charge. I called Kristin's aunt and she and his uncle came to the hospital to support me.

I met another doctor later that day. The doctor informed me that she was so happy to have met me, and she further stated that she now had a clear understanding of his complex medical problems. She also reassured me that he would not be going to a group home. She also agreed that a group home was not the facility for him. The following day, I met the head doctor who came in to check on Kristin. He informed me that Kristin was stabilized, and he could be discharged with services in place for him. On Tuesday, March 17, 2017, Kristin was discharged. Kristin's stepdad and I came and took him home. This entire experience with the social worker trying to send my son to a group home was very heartbreaking to me. As a parent, I know that I must continue to be a strong advocate for my son, even as an adult child. **1 Peter 5:6,7** tells us: *"Humble yourselves therefore under the mighty hands of God, that He may exalt you in due time: Casting your cared upon Him; for He careth for you."*

~4~
Pre-School and Elementary Years

For all of Kristin's early years, he was cared for at home. Because of his complex medical condition, there was no way I could enroll him in a daycare. As a result, I took several leaves of absence from my job to care for him. But the truth remained that I was a single parent of two children and I had to earn a regular and consistent income to support my family. Kristin was very fond of one of his aunts and I felt extremely comfortable with him in her care. So, during the period that I did go to work, his aunt cared for him. As the days, months, and years passed by, I saw my son transform from a baby to a toddler, to a preschooler. While I was happy to see him grow, I dreaded what lay ahead. Many thoughts flooded my mind and I had many sleepless nights fighting with the inevitable. You see, even though he had special needs, he was a child that had needs that grew beyond me. Kristin needed an education and I had to decide whether to send my son to school or to find some way to home school him.

There were countless "what ifs" that plagued me as I considered sending him to school. What if Kristin had an episode in school and needed medical attention? What if the teachers did not know how to deal with his emergency? What if they were not patient with him or sensitive to his special needs? How would his classmates and peers react and interact with him? Was sending him to school a safe or wise decision? These were but a few of the countless unanswered questions that I dealt with. I was full of fear and confusion. My heart cried out to God for direction. I knew that God would lead me in the right direction, because God has never failed me yet. Even though I loved Kristin and was instinctively inclined to protect him, I knew I could not shelter him forever. In addition to gaining an education, he needed to learn how to interact with children and other people outside of his family cycle. So, after much deliberation, faith prevailed over fear. The decision was made for him to attend preschool. **Isaiah 54:17** tells us: *"No weapon that is formed against thee shall prosper; and every tongue that shall rise against thee in judgment thou shalt condemn. This is the heritage of the servants of the Lord, and their righteousness is of me, saith the Lord."*

The time eventually came for me to register him for preschool. His preschool teacher was a very pleasant person and I was quite familiar with her because she was also my first son's preschool teacher. I met with the teacher several times prior to admitting him. During our meeting, we discussed some of Kristin's special needs and I shared with her what signs to look for that might indicate that he was having an episode and needed medical attention. I also gave her all his medical forms and other documents. She in turn provided me with the administrative forms that I had to fill out for his school. I completed all the necessary administrative documentation, submitted the forms to the teacher, and the matter was set. My son was enrolled and ready to attend.

The first day of school came and my heart was overwhelmed as I left Kristin in the hands of his teacher. I was nervous all day and this feeling only subsided when I picked him up at the end of the school day. Every school day felt like an emotional rollercoaster for me. On one hand, I was happy and proud that he was attending school as a normal child his age. On the other hand, I was sad and afraid because I knew that he was not a normal child, and there were so many things that could go wrong with his health. As the days passed, my anxiety dissipated, and it became easier for me to leave him in his teacher's care. I did a lot of volunteer work in his classroom during his preschool year, which allowed me to keep a close eye on him.

As I anticipated, Kristin's preschool years were filled with many health challenges. He was sick quite a lot and had many absences due to several hospitalizations. However, Kristin's medical-compromised conditions were just one of his many challenges. There were social and psychological issues that he also had to deal with. Kristin did not make many friends in preschool and most of his classmates did not play with him. He became a loner, and for the most part he played alongside his classmates or by himself. Due to low blood count (thrombocytopenia), he had to wear a helmet in school to protect his head from any internal injury. I believe this contributed to his isolation because he looked a little strange with the helmet on. Kristin was very conscious about his appearance, and he did not want to be seen in school with the helmet. Every morning when he arrived at school he would cry and beg me not to let him wear the helmet. I was hurt to see him isolated from his peers, and even though it broke my heart, I had to insist that he wear the helmet for his safety. Kristin cried during the entire time in his class as he wore the helmet. Kristin's preschool year was short. He spent only a few months in preschool before moving on to kindergarten.

Kristin was very ill for most of the time during kindergarten. He spent a lot of time in the hospital and attending medical appointments. At school, his kindergarten teacher was wonderful, and she cared for him very much. But again, as in preschool, he struggled during kindergarten and became very unhappy and withdrawn. Kristin was still unable to make friends at school and he played alone most days. He began to struggle to keep up with his school work and he fell behind his classmates. At the end of the school year, after much deliberation, it was determined that he should repeat kindergarten, so he did. Kristin's second year in kindergarten class was not good for him. It was like déjà vu all over again. My son was still a loner and he had no friends. Luckily for Kristin, this year he had a female cousin in the second grade and she would play with him and even defended him when other children picked on him. He still encountered problems keeping up with the school work and this frustrated him. Even as I tried to work with him at home, he still could not comprehend what I was trying to teach him. His inability to grasp kindergarten concepts bothered me a great deal. My heart cried out to God to help me find the root of his problem. I began to think that maybe some of his inability to learn was because of his birth defect.

In the two years that followed, Kristin was placed in a regular first and second grade class. He fell farther and farther behind his classmates. It bothered him that he could not understand his class work. He continued to experience the same social problems. He was still alone, and he had no friends. He became even more withdrawn and lonely. His frustration and anger grew each year. It became apparent that he could not cope on this level and needed special education. I spoke to his second grade teacher. In addition to speaking to her, I wrote a letter to his principal about the problems that he was experiencing. In the letter, I informed the principal that Kristin's needs were not being met. I suggested that he be placed in a smaller class to get the education attention that he needed. In response to my letter, the school scheduled a meeting for Kristin to have an Individual Educational Plan (IEP). Based on our discussion at the meeting and Kristin's IEP results, the school decided that going forward he would be placed in a special class with third, fourth, and fifth graders.

During the third, fourth, and fifth grade years, he was placed in a small learning support class with a group of children with different kinds of special needs. Kristin was a very quiet, frightened, and timid boy. In that class he was teased, even by his own peers who had special needs just like him. Every day when I picked him up from school, he would tell me that the children teased or hit him. This was disturbing to me in the earlier years when he was teased by his peers. I would tell him to ignore the mean words because the children didn't understand what they were saying. But being hit by his classmates... this roused to another level and the abuse towards my son could not be tolerated. I met with his teacher to discuss the abuse that was happening to him by his classmates. His teacher was very nice and explained to me that she needed assistance to help with some of the students. However, the lack of funding prohibited the principal from aiding.

After hearing that there was a lack of funding to help in my son's class, I felt that I had to do something to help the teachers get assistants. I made an appointment to meet with the principal. When I met with her, I discussed the incidents about my son being abused by his peers and the need for having an assistant to help in my son's classroom to decrease any further abuse that my son was experiencing. The principal simply said that she could not help me, and there was no funding for assistants for that class.

The principal's reaction and response to my son's plight confirmed to me what I was thinking all along: there were major changes to be made at Kristin's school and the entire school district was in major need of reformation. I also knew that I had to be an advocate for my son and other children like him. I knew that I had an uphill battle ahead, but I was ready and willing to fight. What I did not know were the challenges that I would face as I fought this battle. I began to research the education system and their approaches to treating children with special needs. By this time, Kristin was almost ready to graduate from elementary school and head onward to middle school.

Sometimes I would imagine Kristin talking to God and asking God, "How will I go through this world of mean and cruel people, being in and out of the hospital and with people who do not understand my disabilities and who see me as an obstacle?" Then I would imagine God talking back to him and saying "You are my precious child, and I gave you a special mother who will love you. There is only one you, and, yes, you are special. Sometimes you may go through difficult times, but I will be there with you. You have a very special gift; the gift of music. You can play the keyboard to perfection. I listen to you when you play the piano. You are wonderfully made, because I made you." Well, now I know that God had a perfect plan for his life.

Kristin was born musically gifted. At two, he would make music with his hands. At three, he started to play the piano and keyboard without any lessons. He would play all the church songs we sang in church, including Beethoven music. God had a vision for me to let other mothers know that it doesn't matter what you see in the natural, God is working it out in the spiritual.

God's Word says, *"What then shall we say to these things? If God is for us, who can be against us?"* (**Romans 8:31**)

~5~

Middle and High School

The first day of school finally arrived and there I was at middle school with Kristin. I hoped and prayed that middle school was going to be better for him. To my dismay, it only got worse. Kristin's nightmares began on day one. Kristin's look of excitement and anticipation quickly changed into tense fear and horror when he saw most of his previous classmates at his middle school. To my surprise and dismay, they were all placed in the same learning support classroom. I soon learned that at this middle school, all special needs children were lumped together in this one class. This time there were children with mental, psychological, and severe behavioral problems. Then there was my son, who had numerous medical problems. On the very first day of school, Kristin was pushed down the stairs by another student and had to be taken to the hospital for treatment. Not long after that incident, he was punched in the mouth by another student and his lip was cut. This caused severe bleeding and his blood count dropped to a very low level. Kristin began to bleed internally and had to be hospitalized. He was traumatized after that incident. At the hospital, he was afraid. He kept saying to me that he didn't want to go back to his school. The look in his eyes was pure fright. My heart cried to God to help him. Psalm 46:11 tells us: "The Lord of hosts is with us; The God of Jacobs is our refuge."

I spent about two years researching how the school system worked and the steps that were needed to get my son's issues heard. Thus, my battle with the school district began. I started by writing letters to some of Kristin's past and present teachers, asking for their support. I wrote letters to the principal, school counselors, the school district, and the Education Law Center. I explained to them that for many years my son had been constantly abused in class by his peers who taunted, teased, and hurt him emotionally, psychologically, and physically. I went on to explain that his special needs were not being met in an overcrowded classroom with only one teacher. I expressed my belief that there was a breakdown in the school system and many times I felt helpless, stressed out, and alone. So, I needed their support to help my son.

Based on the responses I got from my many letters, it seemed that most people were aware of what was happening with the school district and the way my son was being treated. They preferred to ignore it and hoped it would get better by itself. Some of Kristin's teachers responded that they were willing to help me fight for his rights and others were reluctant to help. Some of the teachers did not want to become involved for fear of retaliation for speaking up against the school district.

Nevertheless, I pressed on. For quite some time, I felt that I was not getting through to those in authority. It seemed that my complaints and concerns fell on deaf ears, although I knew that if a parent gave up on a child, that child would be at a disadvantage and probably expect the world to give up on him or her as well. I grew very weary at times. On some occasions, I felt like giving up because I seemed to be hitting brick walls on every turn. But I would often ask myself, "What is going to happen to my child and others like him if I give up?" The answers to my questions were not too far behind. I would hear that still, soft voice telling me to fight for a chance for my son. I knew that I had to keep on moving, pushing forward, and fighting his battle until my voice was heard. So, I continued to fight for my child one way or another. I continued to say to myself, "You must never give up! You cannot give up." I reminded myself of the scripture that says if God is for you then who shall be against you? I knew that I was not in this battle alone and I just needed to allow God to have His way in the situation for me. My heart cried out to God to give me the strength.

God's Word says, *"Look to the Lord and His strength: seek His face always."* (**1 Chronicles 16:11**)

Thank God, we got a breakthrough. The school district agreed to put two assistants in Kristin's classroom. Because of the number of students in his class, two assistants did not improve the situation. The children's special needs were so diverse and complex that it was very difficult for both teachers and aides to manage the classroom. Kristin was still attacked by students. The teacher and the aide give their all but were burnt out trying to meet the needs of all students.

On numerous occasions, I would take time off from my job to do volunteer work in Kristin's class. While it felt great helping in the classroom, it was very traumatic for me to witness Kristin being abused. Many times, I would leave the classroom with him feeling like I had failed him. After volunteering several times in his class, I realized that it would take more teacher and aide support to make a difference. At that point, I began to feel emotionally burdened yet again. On one hand, I was happy and grateful for what was already accomplished. On the other hand, I was sad, stressed out, and frustrated because we hadn't even begun a viable solution to this problem. Like any other child, my son and other children with special needs deserve the right to be in a safe learning environment. They deserve a place where they can focus on acquiring knowledge and experience the normal things that children their age experience, rather than being constantly consumed with fear of abuse and being injured in school.

Clearly there was more to be done. I had more discussions with Kristin's teachers and I wrote letters to the principal concerning Kristin's needs not being met. Whether it was because they didn't know or were simply unwilling to help me any further, the bottom line is – I received zero support from the principal. I saw myself becoming more and more overwhelmed with fury and anger. I knew that being furious and angry wouldn't help my son. I had to make a conscious effort to transform my anger into passion, perseverance, and a strong determination to continue to fight for the changes that were needed in his school. My heart cried out to God to provide me with the wisdom, strength, and resources that I needed to continue to be an advocate for Kristin.

I emerged with a renewed vigor. I was ready to continue my battle and I had a plan of action. I wrote letters to the school district again. This time, I was forthright. I reiterated the conclusion that the education system for special needs children failed them and something had to be done about it as a matter of urgency. I added that my child had the same rights as an individual with disabilities in the United States – to be in a safe, caring, educational environment, according to the IDEA (Individuals with Disabilities Education Act). Psalm 32:8 tells us: "I will instruct thee and teach thee in the way which thou shalt go: I will guide thee with Mine eye."

LAURA BAILEY-AUBOUG

~6~

Letters Advocating For Kristin

In this chapter, you will see a few of the several letters I wrote on behalf of my son. These letters were written so that my son could have the proper care and services to have a successful life both in and out of school.

LETTER #1: To the Principal 11-28-1998

It seems to me that you have shown no interest in the small learning community class I have written to you many times concerning the number of students in that class since September of 1998. You do know that there are twenty students with learning disabilities and only one teacher? From my observation on 11-24-98, some of the children have serious behavioral problems. On 11-16-98, my son was hit repeatedly on his head by a classmate and on 11-23-98, he was kicked off a chair by another classmate. My son fell to the ground and injured his elbow. On 11-24-98, he was stabbed with a pencil under his eye. For all the incidents, he had to seek medical attention. Those incidents could have been avoided had there been an assistant in his class working with his teacher. The children in the small learning community are treated like second-class citizens. At this present time, my son is afraid to go to school and he is having nightmares about his classmates attacking him. My son is eight years old and small built, but his classmates are ten and eleven years old. As a principal, you have failed both my son and me.

Laura Auboug

Kristin Horton's Mother

LETTER #2: To the Middle School Principal 3-18-02

I am very concerned about the overall safety and academic skills of my son Kristin Horton, who is in the 6th grade. My son was injured in school on 2-6-02 by another student. This injury caused him a visit to the emergency room and a follow-up with his primary doctor. For me to be more knowledgeable about the special education program Kristin is enrolled in and avoid any more injuries to my child, I am requesting a re-evaluation be carried out and for me to be present, since I am a member of the multidisciplinary team. My son has numerous medical problems, one of them a bleeding disorder where it is critical that he be protected from any type of injury to his body. At this present time, my son is afraid to return to school. I am extremely worried about his safety in this special education classroom and his safety on the school premises. I am requesting a full written statement of what occurred to my son on 2-6-02 and to meet with the school counselor as soon as possible. I need to discuss other options to avoid further injuries to my child and what changes need to be made to improve the academic year for him. My son has all rights under the IDEA (Individual with Disabilities Education Act).

Your prompt attention to this matter will be greatly appreciated.

Respectfully,

Laura Auboug

Kristin Horton's Mother

LETTER #3: To Principal December 2002

I am concerned about my son Kristin Horton's educational problems he's been having in school. Kristin is a special education student with numerous medical problems. Kristin needs assistance during school hours to help him whenever he is having a difficult time. I would like to request a pre-hearing conference to discuss my concerns about my child.

Laura Auboug

Kristin Horton's Mother

LETTER #4: To his School 9-19-03

I am the parent of Kristin Horton, date of birth 5-6-90. At this present time my son is hospitalized. I feel when he is discharged from the hospital he will need a placement in a private school. I would like his school to conduct all necessary evaluations to determine his need to be placed in a specialized private school upon his discharge.

Thank you,

Laura Auboug

Kristin Horton's Mother

LETTER #5: To the Principal 5-6-04

Dear Principal,

I am Kristin Horton's mother. I am very disturbed to know that my child's IEP is not being implemented by the school. It hurts me very much when he tells me that he is in a classroom without any students. I do appreciate that the school is trying to accommodate him; however, this school cannot meet his needs. I was very upset on 5-3-04 when I brought my son to school and I was told that he could not stay in school because he has no one to work with him. At this present time, my son is in the hospital. He was admitted on May 2, 2004. I need to know that he will have a placement when he comes out from the hospital. I would like the school to consider this. Also, I would like to request a meeting to discuss my child's needs upon his discharge because I do not think that it is fair for him to be in a classroom all alone.

Thank you,

Laura Auboug

Kristin Horton's Mother

LETTER #6: To the School 5-14-04

I am the mother of Kristin Horton, who is registered at this school. At this present time again, he is in the hospital and I would like to update you on Kristin's present condition. He was approved for a private school through the school district. However, a private school has not accepted him at this present time. He was discharged from the hospital on Thursday, April 29th, 2004 with the recommendation from his doctor for a long-term partial hospitalization, while waiting for an approved private school. However, a partial program was not found for him and I was told by his doctor to take him back to his middle school and let the school deal with it. Kristin then returned to his middle school, which could not accommodate him, and he was then admitted back into the hospital. On May 13th, 2004, he was transferred from the hospital to a partial hospitalized program. Now I am very much concerned about his discharge plan since he was discharged previously without an after-care plan. I am requesting that an interagency meeting with all agencies, hospital, and people that are involved with my child's education plan be conducted. Again, I am afraid that my child will be discharged without an after-care plan. Kristin's IEP was written for him and it must be implemented, but as of this present time it has not been implemented. I have had sleepless nights and severe stress due to my son's needs not being met. However, I will not stop seeking help for him. I am Kristin's mother and advocate, and I will not stop until my son's needs are met.

Please inform me of the time and place that this meeting will take place.

Laura Auboug

Kristin Horton's Mother

LETTER #7: Education Director 5-23-04

I am the mother of Kristin Horton, who is currently in a partial hospitalization program. At this present time, I would like to request an independent evaluation for my child.

Thank you,

Kristin Horton's Mother

LETTER #8: To His School, the Hospital, and the Agency 3-9-05

I am the mother of Kristin Horton, who is registered at W. Academy School. At this present time, he is in the hospital in the adolescent unit. I would like to update you on Kristin's present situation. Due to negative side effects from his medication, he had to be hospitalized at Children's Hospital. He was then transferred to another hospital, hoping to meet his complex medical needs. He has missed over thirty days from school. He has numerous medical problems and negative side effects to numerous medicines. He was accepted at a specialized treatment hospital and school in Virginia, where they can meet his needs medically. However, it was not approved for him to receive treatment out of state. I would like an interagency meeting to be conducted between the agencies, hospitals, and people involved with my child's educational plans for my child's needs to be met. I am requesting the meeting to be held at the hospital that he is in presently. I am his mother and advocate, and I will not stop until his needs are met. Please inform me of the day and time of this meeting.

Thank you,

Laura Auboug

Kristin's Horton's Mother

LETTER #9: To: JG Founder and CEO Quality Progression. Copy to: AH Quality Progression Program Director / CP Kristin's Horton Support Coordinator/ Senator Anthony H. Williams / Senator Robert P Casey / President Barrack Obama / DK Program Specialist / B.J Support Coordinator 11-06-2015

Dear Mr. Goldberg,

As of 11-16-2015, my special needs adult son Kristin Horton, DOB 05-06-1990, will be discharged from his day program due to his medical needs for one-to-one support not being met. As Kristin's mother, provider, and advocate, I am reaching out to you desperately for assistance, for a one-to-one service for my son, for him to continue in his day program.

This program has benefited Kristin tremendously in various areas of his life. At the day program, Kristin socialized with others, had learned life skills, and enjoyed outdoor events. Kristin's verbal and physical skills, as well as his independence, had increased at his day program. Prior to Kristin being at the program, I cared for him at home for four years while waiting for Kristin to be accepted into a day program. Unfortunately, all of Kristin's social, emotional, language, cognitive, and physical skills decreased during those four years of waiting for a program to accept him, and Kristin became very withdrawn from society.

I am a mother who is willing to go the extra mile to care for my son. Kristin is a human being, he has emotions, he has feelings, and he has a heart just like you and me. I am pleading with you and all services to help provide Kristin with one-to-one support, so that Kristin can continue to learn and grow in his day program and have the opportunity to live a productive life in our society.

Thank you,

Laura Auboug

Kristin's Horton's Mother

LETTER #10: To: Children's Behavioral Health Services Attn: Dr. K 06/02/2009

I am the mother of the above-referenced name, date of birth 5-6-90. I have had the opportunity of reading Kristin's evaluations by you dated 11-19-08, and 3-26-09. I believe that your evaluation about Kristin focuses on his weakness and you have ignored his strengths. Do you think 10 hours of Therapeutic Support Staff a week can support Kristin emotionally, mentally, behaviorally, and educationally? Do you think Kristin is miraculously going to improve by decreasing his T.S.S.? Kristin may not be a Doctor, Lawyer, or Scientist, but he is gifted in his own way. Kristin is musically gifted. He can play both piano and organ by ear, but he has never had any lessons for both. He participates in the art program at his school on Artsonia. He has won a Hall of Fame Award, on 3-5-09. He has 25 pieces of art in an online gallery, which you can view in the enclosed activity report for him.

You have mentioned in his evaluation that he has no social interaction outside of school, but again you are wrong. Kristin goes to a youth program once a week from 7-9 p.m., he goes to the Y.M.C.A. regularly, and he is scheduled to do volunteer work three times a week for a summer camp, beginning June 24th, 2009. He goes shopping for food of his choice with his parents and also for clothing. You also stated in his evaluation, dated 11-19-08, that in "June I recommended that Kristin's family begin to apply for other services. According to Mr. C, O.M.R. personnel informed him that no such application has yet been made by the family, which is required by this office despite Mr. C's attempt to begin the referral process."

Again, you are wrong, and I don't know where you got that information from. First, Kristin has been registered for services through the O.M.R. and Quality Progression since

2004, two years prior to his services, and enclosed is a copy of his welcome letter from Quality Progressions and letters from O.M.R. dated April and August 2004. Nevertheless, the services that you would like him to receive are not going to be in effect for him until he turns 21 and is out of school. Kristin is still in school. Please take time to review your information and sources; it appears to me that you are receiving false information. My son will continue to work at his own pace and achieve his goals, and no one should put a limit on when he should accomplish a goal. We are all individuals, and we should be treated that way.

Concerned Parent,

Ms. Laura Auboug

My battle with the education system also took a toll on my professional career as a teacher. That same year that I wrote several letters about getting help for Kristin, I continued my employment at a preschool program. The director at my employment was cruel and did not care what was happening to my son. Kristin's school had scheduled him for an IEP (Individual Educational Plan) meeting at 9 a.m. at his school, which was approximately a two-hour ride from my job. One week before my son's IEP meeting, I went to the director and asked her for the time off to attend my son's meeting, but her response was, "Tell your son's teacher to schedule his IEP meeting after 3 p.m." However, IEP meetings are normally scheduled in the morning. From that day on, she began to treat me unkindly and in an unfair way. Well my son's IEP was more important, so therefore I took the time off and was present for my son's IEP meeting. Another time she told me that I could not use the phone to call my son's school nurse. The school nurse had called on my job and left an important message for me at work, to call immediately.

At the end of that year, I wrote various poems dedicated to Kristin, accompanied him to his doctor's appointments, and continued to be his main advocate

LAURA BAILEY-AUBOUG

~7~

Poems For Kristin

MY MELODY

Sweet and gentle you seem to me

Kristin, Kristin, Kristin,

You are a melody

For you are God's

Precious Gift to me.

I WONDER

Sometimes I often wonder What life would really be?

If I didn't have you

And you didn't have me

There would be no you or me

To me you are like a star

That shines in the night

To me you are like the ocean

For us both cannot part

To me you are like a cabbage

Divided into two

He leaves I give to others the heart I give to you

MY SPECIAL CHILD

From the beginning

You were not like other children

I know God was fully aware

He knew how much you can bear

And He knew how much I care

I would give the world away

Just to make your day

My heart wishes you were well

But we must trust in God

And claim that you are well

I BELIEVE

I believe that one day Kristin will recover from his illness

And grow up to be a strong, intelligent man

I believe that through all the trials and tribulations

Kristin will follow the right track

I believe that Kristin will be okay

I believe that Kristin will survive

I believe that Kristin will live a good life

When I put all my belief in GOD, I know that Kristin will achieve

I SCREAM

I scream

I cry

I pray

For a while

Why me, Lord?

What have I done?

You gave me this child

To make me smile

But I feel so sad

When I should be glad

His sickness and pain

Seem to me like a chain

But I know You, my God

Will heal my child's pain All over again and again.

UNIQUE YOU

12 fingers

12 toes

You came into this world

Only God knows

You are like a rose

~8~
Setbacks

My son's last year in middle school was his worst year ever. The struggles began when I tried to advocate for him to be placed in a specialized school. I had to call several inter-agency meetings and invite an advocate from a parent-involved network to assist me. The meeting was held that year in his middle school. To my surprise, I was told that the school district could not provide a safe environment for Kristin due to his multiple medical problems and disabilities. I was informed by the district that he must be placed in a classroom by himself until they decided what they could do for him. I was hurt and devastated. Just the fact that my child would be in a classroom all alone made it heartbreaking for me. That year he was in a classroom all by himself with no other students… just him and a teacher. But I knew that God was with him and that He would comfort him in every circumstance.

God's Word says, "*Blessed be the God and Father of our Lord Jesus Christ, the Father of mercies and God of all comforts, who comforts us in all our tribulation, that we may be able to comfort those who are in any trouble, with the comfort with which we ourselves are comforted by God.*" **(2 Corinthians 1: 3-4)**

After being in a class all by himself for three months, the school suggested that he should be placed on homebound for another three months until they came up with a plan for a specialized school for him. That year he had a private school teacher come to the house to teach him for three months. He was safe and happy with no problems, but because of the breakdown with the school district, he had to return to his middle school in the same classroom where he had been abused. There were thirty children in his classroom and many of the children had special needs.

The first day he returned to his middle school after being homebound for three months, he began to hallucinate and he became very afraid. Right then, I knew that the school district classroom was not working for him because he was too afraid of the children. I believed he had remembered the abuse he endured in that classroom. Several times, he would go into an outburst, scream, and cry. That year he had to be hospitalized for severe depression and other medical problems.

Prior to Kristin's discharge from the hospital, I called an interagency meeting with all those who were involved with his educational plan. I informed them that he would need a specialized school program to meet his needs when he came out from the hospital. The facial expressions of all the people sitting there said, "Who is this crazy mother?" Nonetheless, I didn't mind fighting and getting feisty for my child's right to a safe education program. That year I had many enemies because I refused to settle for less. I refused to allow my son to stay in his unaccommodating school circumstances. After several years of battling the school district, I won the battle and they honored my request to pay for my son to attend a private school. **Philippians 4:19** tells us: *"But my God shall supply all your needs according to His riches in glory by Christ Jesus."*

Upon discharge from the hospital, Kristin began his new private school. It was a beautiful school with lots of space, and even a rose garden. He had wonderful specialized teachers, and all his teachers were educated in the field of Special Education. Kristin also had excellent staff members that cared for him and treated him wonderfully. The director was caring, and it seemed to me that everyone at that school cared about special needs children. That year in his private school was a dream come true for him. He was not afraid to go to school; in fact, he was happy every morning to get ready for his new school. He loved his new school and friends. He made lots of nice friends, and, most of all, he was never hurt at that school. Kristin's wonderful and peaceful time at his private school was approximately seven years. The following year, Kristin continued his battle with numerous medical problems. It seemed that every time he would overcome one barrier, there was another one waiting ahead for him. Yet, I continued to keep the faith that God would always be with him through whatever situations he may go through. I continue to keep God's word deep in my heart. **Isaiah 53:5** tells us: *"But He was wounded for our transgressions; He was bruised for* *our iniquities; The chastisement for our peace was upon Him, And by His stripes we are healed.*"

When Kristin returned to his private school after being in the hospital that year, he enjoyed the rest of his years there. His teachers at the private school were delighted to have him back. His art teacher worked with him on all his artwork, for which he received many awards. Kristin also has a website to purchase all his artwork on various items: T-shirts, mugs, aprons, etc. God uses Kristin's gift of creativity. To God be the glory.

In 2011, when Kristin graduated from high school and it was the best year for him, he had a wonderful graduation at his school and a wonderful graduation party at home. All his family members were present. He also had friends at his party and his godmother, who loves him dearly.

~9~
The Family Life and Holidays

Kristin loves both his grandparents very much. His grandmother helped cared for him, and his grandfather has always been special in his life. Kristin's grandmother battled Parkinson's Disease for several years. Whenever I took Kristin over to visit her, his grandmother would use her hands and whatever little strength she had left in her body to pray for him. Kristin's grandmother would always remind me to continue to pray for Kristin and anoint him every night. Sadly, on Thanksgiving morning 2012, Kristin's grandmother passed away. Kristin was saddened, and so was the entire family. Kristin's grandfather was also close to him. Kristin was his grandfather's "sidekick." Kristin's grandfather would tell me that he and Kristin had a lot in common. Whenever my dad would come over to my house, Kristin would dance for him. His grandfather would laugh with Kristin. Kristin's grandfather would sit out on the porch with him while they both listened to music. His grandfather got very ill and he passed away on August 21, 2016. Three days before he passed away, Kristin and his stepdad went to visit his grandfather. As his grandfather laid helpless on the bed, when his stepdad mentioned that Kristin was here to visit him, Kristin's grandfather stood up on his bed and said to Kristin, "Oh Oh!! Look at my boy!" Those were the last words that his grandfather spoke to Kristin.

Throughout Kristin's life, his family members were always there for him, and Kristin loves his younger cousins. Nevertheless, his younger cousins would try to make him tough by provoking him, and Kristin would often get upset and cry. Although I knew that it was typical cousin rivalry, I was always ready to defend him. During family gatherings, his younger cousins would play rough with him and he would cry. His younger cousin would always tell him he must learn to fight back and stop being so afraid. I would always get into arguments with his aunts about his younger cousins trying to make him tough. I never got any satisfaction from his aunt because his aunt claimed that he needed to defend himself. She would always tell him that he must defend himself, and not to let anyone push him around, not even his cousins. But Kristin was timid and afraid of his younger cousin, and she reminded him of the children in his school that bullied him. So, he never fought back. I think that his younger cousin provoked him because she wanted him to fight back and learn to defend himself.

On one of our Fourth of July celebrations, the family was in the park and Kristin was playing by himself when his younger cousin who has always tried to make him tough hit him. Suddenly, he came crying to me, telling me what his cousin did to him. Well, that started an argument that quickly escalated between his aunt and me. I tried to explain to his aunt that Kristin had always been picked on, hit on, and teased and bullied in school from a young age and he should not have to go through this bullying when he was around his family. I don't think that his aunt understood what I was trying to explain to her. However, she never saw him as helpless, defenseless, and being bullied the way I saw him. During another instance, Kristin was over at his aunt's house. Some of his cousins were playing in the street and some of them were riding bikes. When Kristin picked a bike up to ride it, his younger cousin, who always tried to make him tough, ran to another cousin and said, "Look, Kristin is riding your bike. Go and take your bike from him. Let's see what he will do." I just looked at both his cousins and shook my head because I knew that they wouldn't recognize the pain they were inflicting on him because they were younger than him, and they were just being typical young cousins.

Kristin's big brothers were wonderful to him. They love Kristin very much. One of his brothers, Christopher, would take him to many of his appointments and would sit in on his many IEP (Individual Education Plan) meetings. He has always been there for Kristin and Kristin loves him. He took him to school, to the park, and to the movies. He always made time to spend with him. He was like his second daddy. However, sometimes Kristin would get upset when his brother corrected him when he did something wrong. Kristin also loves and respects his step-brother, Carl, who takes him on long rides around the city. He would hang out with his step-brother's friends, play basketball, and watch movies.

From the time Kristin's stepdad came into his life, when he was three years old, they bonded. His stepdad loves Kristin dearly. He has always been active in his life. He attended important school meetings, took him on vacations and daily outdoor events. They both love to go driving to the airport. Kristin enjoys when his stepdad shows him the planes descending and taking off. Kristin gets excited about planes, and his stepdad loves to see him get excited. They also go for longs drives to the malls, to the parks, and to South Street, which is one of Kristin's favorite places. Once a week his stepdad takes him to the car auction. When Kristin arrives at the auction, he walks around giving everyone a "high-five." Kristin loves to watch the people bet on the cars. On several occasions, his stepdad would take him for a ride in the auction cars, and sometimes Kristin would choose the trucks. Kristin also enjoys going with his stepdad to visit friends, and working on cars.

Kristin's stepdad has proven to be more than a stepdad to him. He has all the qualities of a wonderful, terrific, compassionate, wonderful dad, and no one on this earth can tell Kristin that he is not his daddy. Kristin would put on his shoes and coat and say to him, "I am ready to go out." Although Kristin's stepdad used to work at night, before he ventured out to his job he would stop at Kristin's room to let him know that he was going to work, and that he would see him in the morning. Then Kristin would wake up early in the morning just to see his stepdad come in from work. When he got home, Kristin would tell him what he wanted for breakfast and he would make it for him. On many occasions, Kristin would say that he wanted pizza and his stepdad would take him to get it. Kristin and his stepdad have such a beautiful relationship.

Kristin has an aunt that was always there for him. One year when Kristin was in Children's Hospital, his aunt left his uncle's 50th birthday party to bring Kristin some food. It was so funny to see her with a long gown, heels, and hair combed up, roaming the hospital and trying to locate Kristin's hospital room just to give him food. After she left the hospital personnel, I laughed. I knew that she was very tired walking around with her heels on, but she did it for her nephew. Kristin's other aunt that he loves very much would call to find out how he was doing. On many occasions, when she would come over to my house, Kristin enjoyed watching television with her, and he would call her name repeatedly. Most times, she would stay at my house with him when I had to venture out.

During the years when Kristin was in a hospital in Virginia, I was worried that he would not get to see his family. But those close to him took time to make the trip to see him. My brother's wife visited Kristin not once but both times he was in Virginia. She would even bring his little cousin to see him. His aunt on his father's side also came to visit Kristin. She brought her two daughters with her. I told his aunts about a joke Kristin played on his grandfather.

Well, the family knew that Kristin likes to play tricks on people. One day, Kristin's grandfather was babysitting him while I was at work (caring for Kristin was a bit scary for his grandfather because of Kristin's numerous medical conditions). Kristin decided to play a trick on his grandfather. He opened the front door and hid under the table while his grandfather was in the bathroom. When his grandfather came out of the bathroom and didn't see Kristin, he noticed that the front door was opened wide. His grandfather ran down the street calling Kristin's name. After his grandfather searched outside and all over the neighborhood, he came and searched inside but there was no Kristin to be found. Suddenly, he heard laughter and it was Kristin laughing at him from under the table. When I arrived at his grandfather's house, his grandfather was in tears. Kristin thought he was being funny by hiding under the table, but I didn't find anything funny about it.

Christmas and holidays were very touching and heartbreaking for me, especially when he was in the hospital in Virginia. When I visited his aunt's home for the Christmas holiday, they were all giving presents to the family for the holidays. I remember vividly as the presents were given out not only to Kristin's cousins, but to friends, their friends' children, and their friend's grandchildren. I noticed his aunt did not have a present for Kristin. I guess because of all the excitement about Christmas and because Kristin was in the hospital for such a long time in Virginia, I can see how she could have forgotten. When I was leaving from her house she called me, and she gave me two Christmas gifts for Kristin. (I thought she had forgotten about Kristin but she did not.) When January 1st came, I was very much stressed out because I had to face the thought of spending a new year without Kristin. I was heartbroken, I was saddened, but God gave me comfort whenever my heart cried out. His word says:

"*I will not leave you as orphans; I will come to you.*" (**John 14:18**)

Kristin stayed in the hospital in Virginia for another seven months. And during those seven months, his stepdad and I visited him weekly. In April of 2006, he was discharged. That day was one of the happiest days I had during that year.

God's Word says, "*You will show me the path of life; In Your presence is fullness of joy; At Your right hand are pleasures forevermore.*" (**Psalm 16:11**)

One of Kristin's fun vacations was his trip to Canada. The trip was a nine-hour drive, and Kristin enjoyed the music and the ride. He also enjoyed the times that we stopped for food. His favorite food was pizza. When we got into Canada we stopped at the Canadian Niagara Falls. Kristin was so amazed to see the water flowing and he kept laughing at the falls and pointing to it. The drive from the falls to Toronto was approximately two hours. When we got into Toronto, Kristin was tired, so we decided to visit his step-aunt in Toronto. Canada was fun for Kristin. He had the opportunity to go shopping in the malls with his step-aunt and family. Kristin took a lot of pictures in Canada. When we got back to Philadelphia from Toronto, Kristin told his family all about the fun time he had in Toronto.

In the year 2012, Kristin had the opportunity to go to the mountains for two weeks. He was very excited to go. Prior to the visit to the mountains, his step-father and I drove him for a one-day visit to the Poconos. It was fun for Kristin. It was something different for him to get away from Philadelphia and venture out to the Poconos. When we got to the site, Kristin jumped out of the car and began to explore the environment. The tour lady took Kristin and us to see his cabin. Kristin was so excited that he walked around the cabin with laughter on his face. I knew that Kristin would love this place since he likes the outdoor environment. When our visit was over, Kristin had a very sad look on his face. I reassured him that he would be coming back very soon.

After a week from that visit, it was time for Kristin to go the Poconos again, this time for two weeks. When we got to the Poconos again, Kristin jumped out of the car and waved goodbye to both his stepdad and me. I was sad, but he was so happy that I could not let him see my sadness. As we drove away, the look on Kristin's face made me smile. He was so happy to be there, so full of joy, so full of life.

Kristin spent two weeks in the Poconos. When the day finally came to pick him up, he was excited about his adventures. Some of Kristin's activities included: horseback riding, swimming, art, music, dance, outdoor fire lighting, and his experience was a brand new adventure for him. He truly came back refreshed and brand new with laughter on his face. For the rest of the year, Kristin traveled with both me and his stepdad, and he surely had a wonderful year.

For the end of the year 2012, Kristin's year ended wonderfully. In September, he had a wonderful staff that took him almost everywhere. Kristin visited the malls, the airport, the movies, and the parks with his staff. He had a tight-knit connection with his staff. During the holidays, Kristin spent time with his family on lots of outdoor events. Kristin danced and sang for his family, which made them laugh. Kristin played sports and rode bikes with his family. December of 2012, his step-aunt came and spent the Christmas holiday with us. Kristin had fun talking and socializing with her. He also danced for her, which made him happy.

The year 2013, Kristin got prepared for another adventurous outing. He went to the Poconos again, this time one weekend in March. He also went in April, May, and two weeks in July. He was so excited about this adventure. Kristin also had a new staff to take him out on weekends and during the week. He was very happy and excited about the beginning of the year of 2013. Kristin's artwork is still being sold on the internet in various items like T-shirts, mugs, handbags, aprons, cooking boards, and other items. He continues to love the Lord and attend church.

In 2014-2015 Kristin's health was great. He was enrolled in a "skilled program," which he enjoyed. Then he was later discharged due to lack of funding. I immediately had to advocate again for my son. I wrote a letter to President Obama, letters to the Senator, and to various agencies requesting funding for the program in which my son was enrolled. In response to my letters, I received two letters from the Office of Presidential Correspondence, which informed me that they would forward my concerns to government agencies. I also received several telephone calls from the Senator's office and was given the appropriate website for further assistance.

On 10-09-2017, Kristin got the victory, and **Philippians 4:6,7** tells us: *"Be careful for nothing, but in everything by prayer and supplication with thanksgiving let your request be made known unto God. And the peace of God, which passeth all understanding, shall keep your hearts and minds through Christ Jesus."* God made a way for Kristin to go into an Intensive Care Facility. Prior to being admitted to the facility, Kristin visited the facility several times, and on some occasion, he had an overnight stay. Today Kristin is at that facility, and he truly enjoys the new environment. Kristin has a one-to-one staff that takes him out daily, and he goes to the mall, movies, dances, and concerts. Every Sunday morning, his staff brings him to fellowship with his church family. Kristin sings and dances in church and he enjoys the attention that he gets from his pastors and church members. Kristin's aunt and cousin come and visit him every Friday at his house. His aunt and cousin bring games and food and they play music with him. Kristin's brother visits every week and his stepdad also visits him and takes him out frequently through the week. Kristin continues to enjoy the attention that he gets from his family.

Today, Kristin continues his fight with this complex medical problem. He has come a very long way. Kristin continues to strive and enjoy family and life events. He enjoys going to our yearly family reunion, where he gets lots of attention. Kristin has been invited to all his cousins', uncles', and aunts' events. Kristin loves all his family and they all love him very much. He draws, plays the keyboard, and enjoys outdoor events. He loves to take rides to the airport and watch the planes depart. We are hoping and keeping the faith for a cure to his complex medical condition. I will continue to trust God because God's word says: "*And this is the confidence that we have in Him, that if we ask any thing according to His will, He hearth us: And if we know that He hears us whatsoever we ask, we know that we have the petitions that we desire of Him.*" **(John 5:14)**

LAURA BAILEY-AUBOUG

Mother's Message

Every time I think about my son Kristin, I think of the many children in the world who were born like him and other children born with special needs. I also think about the parents who are faced with the challenging medical, psychological, and social problems that I still face daily.

To all parents who have a child that was born with numerous disabilities, for the parents who have been through the struggles of fighting for an appropriate education program for your child. For all the parents who have been through requesting interagency meetings so that your child's need can be met. For all the parents who have been through the stress and frustration of writing letters and advocating for your child; you are not alone. I know the pain you feel inside. I know the hurt of not having your child's needs met and God knows it too.

You want your child to be in a safe education environment to learn and grow. You want your child to be loved by others, to be treated fairly, and to be accepted by society. You must not give up on your child; be an advocate for your child. It is not going to be easy, but God will give you the strength to fight any battle.

Remember that your struggles of today will help you to develop your strength for tomorrow. Hold on to God's hands and never let go. One day, you and your child will have the victory. 1 Corinthians 15:57 tells us: *"But thanks be to God who gives us the victory through our Lord Jesus Christ."* Just keep the faith in Jesus Christ's name. God is with you and you can ride out the storm. Just continue to be an advocate for your child. Hold on; you can make a difference in your child's life. Don't ever give up on your child, and remember that whatever situation that you may be in, continue to trust God, and He will never have failed you.

"For we walk by faith not by sight." (**2 Cor.5:17**)

KRISTIN GALLERY

LAURA BAILEY-AUBOUG

Kristin's Timeline

My Miracle

LAURA BAILEY-AUBOUG

A Great day at church

Kristin, you have been a blessing from the start.

I love you my son with all my heart.

Love Mom.

MY HEART CRIES OUT

Author Laura Bailey-Auboug

About The Author

Laura Bailey-Auboug is a native of Trinidad and Tobago West Indies. She immigrated to the United States in February 1980, where she met and married her husband Yves Auboug in 1999. She holds a BA in Education and an MA in Special Education. She is the mother of two biological sons, Christopher and Kristin, and two stepchildren, Danielle and Carl. She has seven grandchildren. She is currently employed as a Special Education teacher with the school district, and volunteers as an advocate for special needs children and parents. She believes that all children are reachable and teachable. Her heart's desire is for all special needs children to be treated fairly, to receive the proper services that they need, to live happily in this society, and to not be discriminated against due to their disability. She began this book in 1992 when her son was diagnosed with DiGeorge's syndrome and multiples disabilities.

Contact Information Laura Bailey-Auboug:

lauboug@eastern.edu

www.ingramcontent.com/pod-product-compliance
Lightning Source LLC
Chambersburg PA
CBHW042336150426
43195CB00001B/13